For Paddy, Conn, Sadie, Ted, and curious minds everywhere. —H.M.

To my three loves: Jery, Harper, and Emerson. —S.H.

Text copyright © 2024 Henry Martin
Illustrations copyright © 2024 Shelley Hampe

Book design by Melissa Nelson Greenberg
These images were created using found paper, acrylic paint, pencils, colored pencils, ink, and compiled digitally.

Published in 2024 by CAMERON KIDS, an imprint of ABRAMS. All rights reserved. No portion of this book may be reproduced, stored in a retrieval system, or transmitted in any form or by any means, mechanical, electronic, photocopying, recording, or otherwise, without written permission from the publisher.

Library of Congress Control Number: 2023947344
ISBN: 978-1-949480-53-5

Printed in China

10 9 8 7 6 5 4 3 2 1

CAMERON KIDS books are available at special discounts when purchased in quantity for premiums and promotions as well as fundraising or educational use. Special editions can also be created to specifications. For details, contact specialsales@abramsbooks.com or the address below.

ABRAMS The Art of Books
195 Broadway, New York, NY 10007
abramsbooks.com

HOW TO LOVE THE WHOLE WORLD

A Story About Artist Agnes Martin

by Henry Martin   art by Shelley Hampe

cameron kids

Agnes Martin loved the whole world.

She loved
the cotton candy–pink dawn

and an eggshell-blue dusk.

Agnes loved
the sea and the river.
She loved trees, roses, the overlooked weeds.

She loved waves.

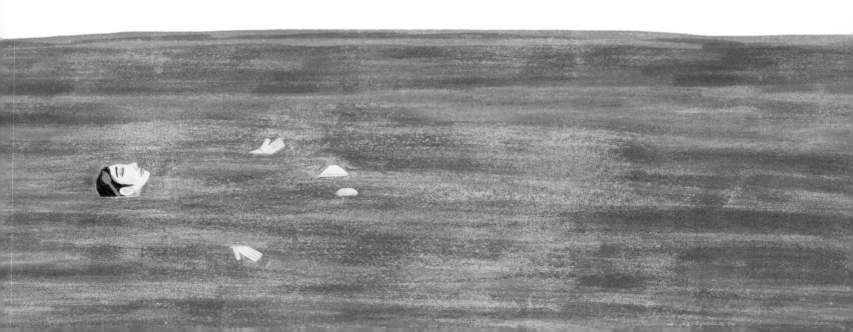

Today I feel happiness.
Today I feel gratitude.
Today I love the whole world.

Agnes loved shapes, too,
and the ordinary line that creates them.

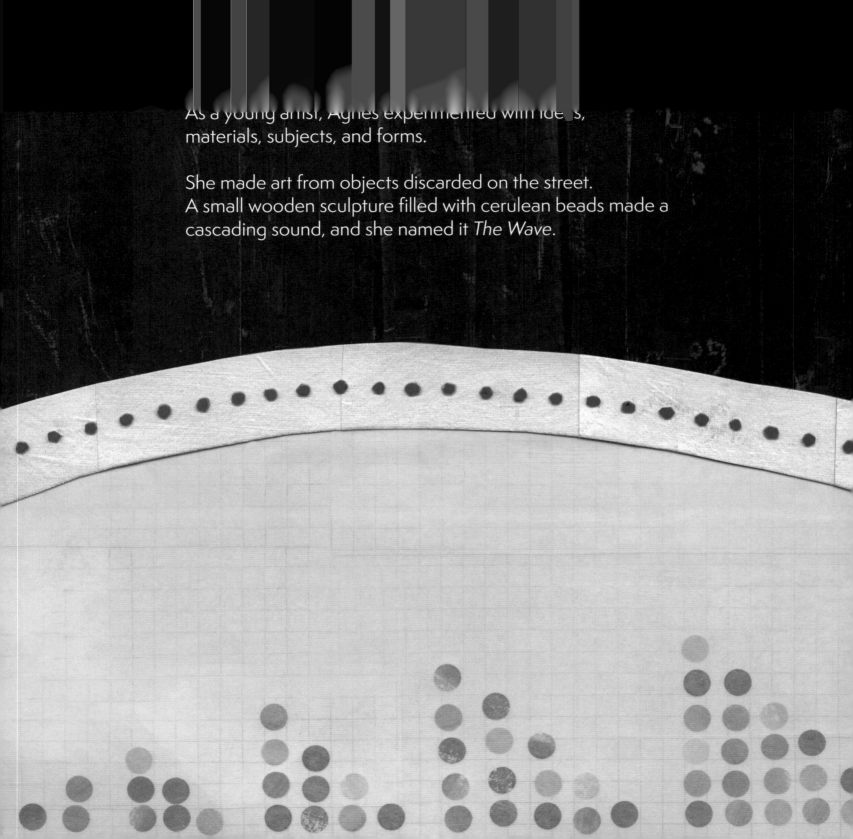

As a young artist, Agnes experimented with ideas,
materials, subjects, and forms.

She made art from objects discarded on the street.
A small wooden sculpture filled with cerulean beads made a
cascading sound, and she named it *The Wave*.

But Agnes did not love all her early artworks, and every year she put many into a bonfire.

Today I feel frustrated.
Today I feel insecure.
Today I do not love the whole world.

When Agnes felt this way, she stopped painting and went on a journey.

She followed the ordinary line of the horizon to
the island of Manhattan,
the Arabian Sea,
the New Mexican desert . . .

and she meditated on what she loved.

If I paint the things I love, then my paintings will be about love, and you will feel love when you look at them.

Agnes pulled a piece of string across a large gesso-painted canvas.
With her pencil she traced the ordinary line from one side to the other.

But there is no such thing as an ordinary line.

A thick, fast, straight line portrays confidence.
A thin, slow, quavering line communicates uncertainty.
A line on its own is loneliness.
Two lines touching are a friendship.
Many lines converging symbolize community.

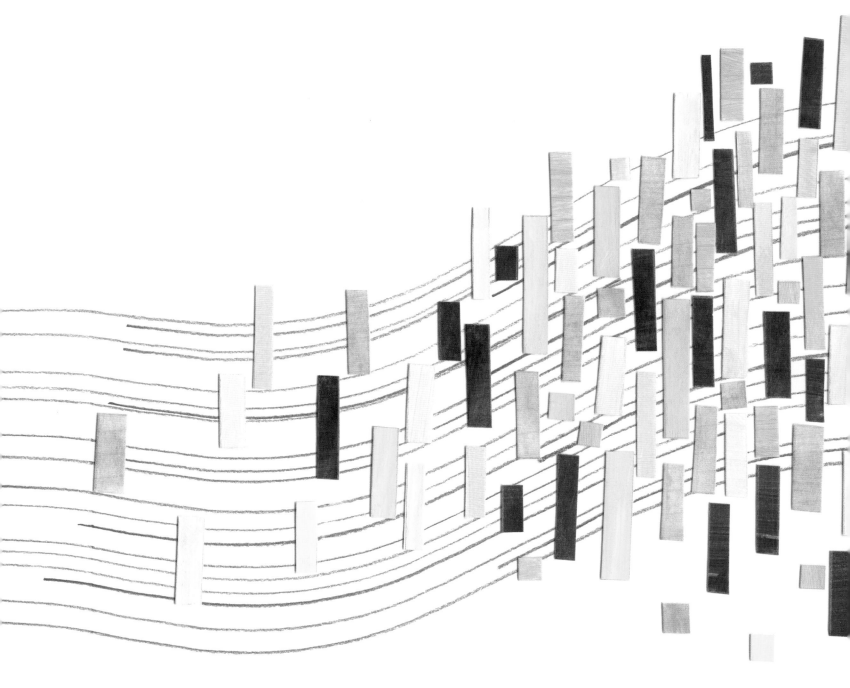

Agnes painted the ordinary line she loved and made it extraordinary.

The more she drew that line, the more joy Agnes felt. First, she thought it was like the sea . . . then she thought it was like singing!

Agnes added so many lines that her paintings became grids composed of thousands of tiny squares or rectangles.

Some grids were blue,
like one named *Night Sea*,
and some pink.
Some grids shimmered
with delicate gold.

Not everybody liked Agnes's new art.

"They are just ordinary lines!"

"These paintings don't even have names!"

"There are no objects!"

"A work of art doesn't have a subject; it has a spirit," Agnes replied, defending her paintings.

On such days, Agnes forgot how to love the whole world.

Today I feel angry.
Today I feel sad.
Today I do not love the whole world.

Agnes believed it would be easier to protect her joy by being alone, and for long stretches of time, she chose to live in solitude.

But it is very hard to love the whole world when you turn your back on it.

One day, Agnes saw children playing hopscotch.

The lines on the pavement reminded her of her grid paintings.

One child sat alone, their back to the others. After some time, the child was invited to join the game, and their face danced with happiness.

That's when Agnes had the thought:

My paintings are like hopscotch. People can drop their troubles into them, rediscover happiness, and love the whole world again.

Agnes's ordered and controlled grid paintings of joy became translucent and expansive band paintings of happiness.

"Wave upon wave," she repeated when she painted her feelings on her canvas. *Gratitude. Affection. Love . . .*

I Love the Whole World.

Agnes had so much love for the world she painted it twice.

Agnes loved painting waves, but she loved the waves of the sea even more.

"It is better to go to the beach and think about painting than it is to be painting and thinking about going to the beach," she said.

To love the whole world is to be in the world.

Light stippling the surf.
Salt in the air.
Sand between toes.
Love and belonging washing over you.
Wave upon wave upon wave.

Today I feel happiness.
Today I feel joy.
Today I love the whole world.

ABOUT AGNES MARTIN

Agnes Martin was a Canadian American artist known for subtle, abstract paintings of grids and bands.

Agnes wrote, "My work is not what is seen. It is what is known forever in the mind." By dispensing with objects, narratives, perspectives, colors, and movement, Agnes invites the viewer to meditate on the simplified purity of what remains: textures, grooves, brushstrokes, and patterns.

Not everybody understood Agnes. Some people considered her different and difficult. Agnes gave away her possessions and paintings; she had girlfriends instead of boyfriends; she was competitive and determined; and she heard voices in her mind. As a result, Agnes was made to feel that her unique qualities, like her unique paintings, were problems to criticize instead of attributes to accept and support.

Eventually, Agnes and her paintings were embraced by the world, and both enjoyed success and respect. Although Agnes had been poor for much of her life, in older age she became wealthy and donated money to social causes in New Mexico. She funded a swimming pool, community center, skateboard park, nature preserve, and charities that helped children and women.

In 1997 Agnes was awarded the Golden Lion at the Venice Biennale in Italy, one of the art world's highest honors, and in 1998 President Bill Clinton presented her with the National Medal of Arts. "Spare and luminous, her works reflect her vision of happiness and beauty," her certificate said, ". . . she is held in the highest regard by her fellow painters."

Museums and collectors around the world rushed to buy Agnes's work, giving Agnes a reputation to equal that of Georgia O'Keeffe, Louise Bourgeois, and Frida Kahlo. In 2018 a large-scale museum retrospective of her work toured London, Düsseldorf, New York, and Los Angeles, inspiring millions.

Agnes believed in accepting and encouraging children for who they are. We hope this book continues this tradition and shines a light on a unique person who achieved, though sometimes struggled to find, peace and happiness in life.

Photo copyright © J. Paul Getty Trust • Martin, Agnes, 1973
Liberman, Alexander and Martin, Agnes • Getty Research Institute, Los Angeles (2000.R.19)

PAINTINGS & ARTWORKS BY AGNES MARTIN MENTIONED IN THE STORY

The Sea, 2003, private collection
The River, 1965, private collection
The Tree, 1964, Museum of Modern Art, New York
The Rose, 1964, Art Gallery of Ontario, Canada
The Rose, 1965, Philadelphia Museum of Art
Rose, 1966, Peggy Guggenheim Collection, Venice, Italy
Weeds, 1963, Robert Elkon Gallery, New York
Happiness, 1999, Dia Art Foundation, New York
Song, 1967, private collection
Night Sea, 1963, San Francisco Museum of Modern Art
Friendship, 1963, Museum of Modern Art, New York
Gratitude, 2001, private collection
I Love the Whole World, 1999, private collection
I Love the Whole World, 2000, Artworkers Retirement Society
The Wave, 1963, Katherine Kaim Kitchen
Affection, 2001, private collection
Love, 1999, Dia Art Foundation, New York
Beach, 1958, private collection, San Francisco

QUOTES & ANECDOTES

"A work of art doesn't have a subject; it has a spirit," from Michael Auping, *30 Years: Interviews and Outtakes* (Fort Worth, TX: Modern Art Museum of Fort Worth, 2007), 223.

"Wave upon wave . . ." from Agnes Martin to Lenore Tawney, July 26, 1965, Lenore G. Tawney Foundation Archives, New York.

"Everything, everything is about feeling . . . feeling and recognition," from John Gruen, "'What We Make, Is What We Feel': Agnes Martin on Her Meditative Practice," *ARTnews*, September 1976, 94.

Hopscotch anecdote from Agnes Martin, interview by Marcia Oliver.

"It is better to go to the beach and think about painting than it is to be painting and thinking about going to the beach . . ." from Agnes Martin, "The Skowhegan Lecture" (lecture, Skowhegan School of Painting & Sculpture, July 3, 1987).

SOURCES
Agnes Martin: Before the Grid, directed by Kathleen Brennan (Kathleen Brennan Studio, 2016).
Agnes Martin, *Writings/Schriften*, ed. Dieter Schwartz (Berlin: Hatje Cantz Publishers, 1998).
Arne Glimcher, *Agnes Martin: Paintings, Writings, Remembrances* (New York: Phaidon Press, 2012).
Barbara Haskell, *Agnes Martin* (New York: Abrams, 1992).
Benita Eisler, "Life Lines," *New Yorker*, 25 January 1993.
Henry Martin, *Agnes Martin: Pioneer, Painter, Icon* (Tuscon, AZ: Schaffner Press, 2018).
Jill Johnston, "Agnes Martin: Surrender and Solitude," in *Gullibles Travels: Writing by Jill Johnston* (New York: Links, 1974).